9/30/00

Dear Diane,

Laughter is truly the best medicine! Enjoy—

Love,

Adrienne

Other Helen Exley Giftbooks:
Men! By Women
The Wicked Little Book of Quotes
The Best of Women's Quotations
Cat Quips

First published in the UK in 1984 by Exley Publications Ltd.
This edition published simultaneously in 1998 by Exley Publications
Ltd in the UK, and Exley Publications LLC in the USA.
© Faith Hines, 1984 (text)
© Gray Jolliffe, 1984 (illustrations)

*Special thanks go to Pam Brown, for her
invaluable help in writing this book.*

12 11 10 9 8 7 6 5 4 3

Edited by Helen Exley
ISBN: 1-86187-106-6

A copy of the CIP data is available from the British Library on request.

Printed in Hungary.

Exley Publications Ltd, 16 Chalk Hill, Watford,
Herts WD1 4BN, UK.
Exley Publications LLC, 232 Madison Avenue,
Suite 1206, NY 10016, USA.

Ms MURPHY'S LAW:
IF ANYTHING CAN GO WRONG IT WILL - AND WHEN IT DOES IT WILL BE THE WOMAN WHO GETS THE BLAME!

Mother Murphology

JENNY'S BASIC LAW OF CONCEPTION
Book the trip of a lifetime.
You will be pregnant before the tickets arrive.

MRS FLAHERTY'S LAWS OF THE BULGE
1. No woman ever believes she's going to get that big.
2. There will come a point when even the most expensive maternity dress will look like a sheet slung over a beach ball.

MRS BROWN'S ALL-ENCOMPASSING LAW OF CHILD-BEARING
Pregnancy is nothing at all like the book.

PENNY'S LAW OF TIMING
The mother-to-be who has made elaborate and efficient arrangements to have the baby at home, will start contractions in the obstetrician's office.

ABSOLUTE LAW OF POSITION
The position most recommended by the medical profession in the delivery of a baby is Flat On Your Back. This is based on the observation that a turtle in this posture is absolutely helpless.

LAW OF PARTURITION
An extensive command of the English language
normally facilitates delivery.

MRS WRIGHT'S ERRATUM

In the books you'd be in bed embowered in blossoms.

In fact, you are in your bathrobe clearing up the poached egg your two-year-old dropped on the kitchen floor.

TWO EARLY PRECEPTS

1. Childbirth has the euphoria of a first night. Parenthood, however, runs as long as a hit musical. With no cast changes.
2. The mother who is planning how she will bring up her baby is looking down at a baby planning how to bring up Mother.

RULE OF THE FIRST NIGHT HOME

There is only one thing that worries a mother more than a crying baby and that is a sleeping baby.

LAWS OF THE BROKEN NIGHT

1. It is inadvisable to put your head around your child's door to check if she is asleep. She was.
2. The baby up the street sleeps through the night.

MRS READY'S LAW OF FIRST THINGS

Most new babies look like rubber gnomes. Most new mothers, on first sight of their offspring, realize they are not natural mothers.

POTTY LORE

A deeply thoughtful baby means dirty pampers.
The baby with the victorious smile is the baby with the bone-dry potty.
The two-year-old who makes it to the potty is too triumphant to remember her panties.
Any baby can time a poop to coincide with the ignition key being turned.

MRS BROWN'S DICTUM

Any mother with only two arms is handicapped.

Mother Murphy and the little Murphies

MRS BROWN'S BASIC LAWS OF CHILDREN

1. Just because they can't say it, doesn't mean they can't do it.
2. Never say anything in front of a child, however young, that can subsequently be used against you.
3. An innocent-looking child is a child up to something.
4. If he comes round the door blowing kisses, count to ten and then go and find out what he's broken.

FAITH'S TWO LAWS
FOR THE DESPAIRING MOTHER

1. No child is as innocent as it looks.
2. It is impossible to make anything childproof.

THREE RULES OF THE GAME

1. The expensive educational toy is the one at the bottom of the toy box.
2. The toy the educationalists condemn is the one they love the best. Probably a gun.
3. People who give your child drums, electronic games or indoor archery sets are childless. Or sadists.

MRS PITT'S CALCULATION

It is possible to tell the age of the children of a house by the height of breakable objects from the floor.

MOTHER PITT'S OBSERVATION

Small children like to do the tidying. The toilet bowl is a popular place for tidying things into.

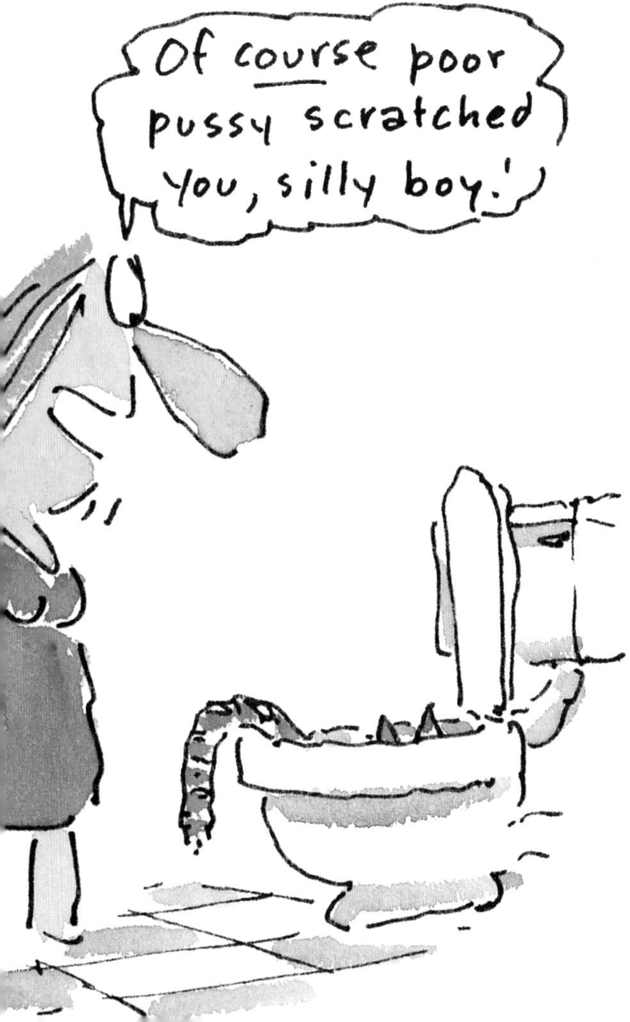
'Of course poor pussy scratched you, silly boy.'

LAW OF THE MOST EXPENSIVE TOY

Toddlers never use the Avon play lipstick.
Only the Estée Lauder.

MRS FINKELSTEIN'S LAWS
OF CREATIVE PLAY

1. The more stimulating the shade of
   paint/crayons/pencils, the less easy they
   are to remove from everything the child
   was wearing.
2. The psychological good done to a child by
   any activity is in direct proportion to
   the permanent psychological harm done to
   its parents.

MRS BANNISTER'S FOUR-POINT
MOBILITY LAW

The child on the tricycle will want
to walk.
The child in the stroller will
want to get out.
The child on foot will want
to get back in the stroller.
The child with the pull-a-long
elephant will insist on riding it.

MRS ALBERTSON'S LORE
The angle of incline increases
in direct proportion to the
number of children
you're pushing.

MOTHER'S LAWS OF ROUTINE

1. A day with children is routine fitted-in loosely around a packed itinerary of the unexpected.
2. Any mother can work like a slave all day – only to welcome her husband home to chaos.

MRS APPLETON'S LAWS OF THE DAY OUT

1. The mother of one finds a babysitter. The mother of four takes her children with her.
2. Every five minutes delay in picking up your child from your friend's home erodes the friendship further.

LINCOLN'S OBSERVATION

All mothers in calling one of their children will work their way through the names of all the others first. This is sometimes extended to the cat.

PAM BROWN'S BASIC LAW OF STAYING AT HOME

Any plan to go anywhere can be thwarted or amended.

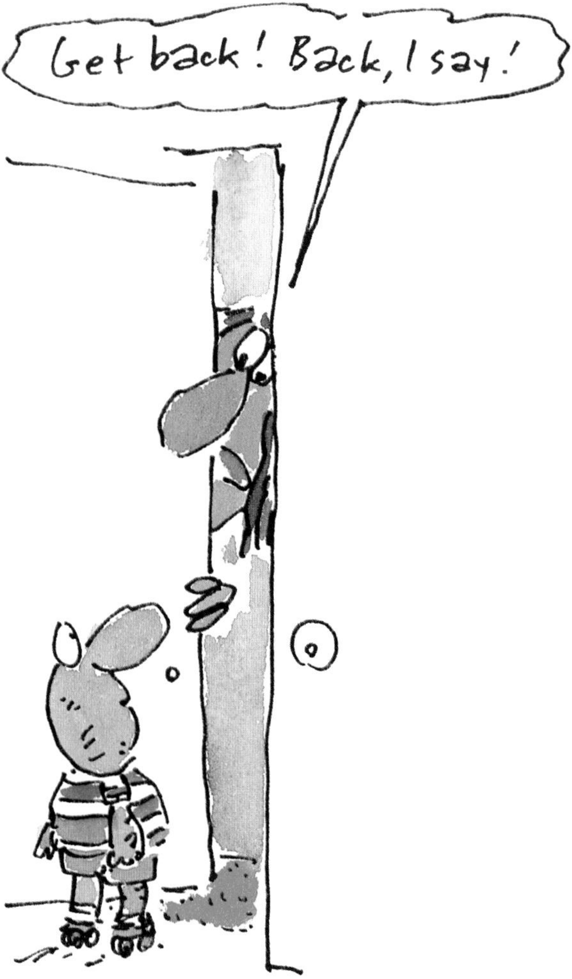
Get back! Back, I say!

MRS GREGORY'S LAW OF SOLID MEMORIES

What starts as a teddy bear apiece ends in an attic full of things your children are saving for their children.

You will be required to store their property until they are married and have attics of their own.

JENNY'S COROLLARY

The day you get the last of your children's clutter into the attic, your eldest daughter announces she is pregnant.

PAM BROWN'S LAW OF MOTHER LOVE

Mother love reaches its highest point when awaiting the return of a child from school, college, a trip abroad or a distant married home. It returns to normal levels approximately five minutes later.

KATY JENKIN'S KEEP-YOUR-COOL LAW

The woman who scolds her child as she repairs the lining of its coat will find she has done a good, neat, tight job of sewing up the armholes.

MRS FREUD'S PSYCHOLOGICAL APPROACH

The only trouble with manuals on child-raising written by experts is that in ten years the experts admit they have changed their minds.

MOTHER'S TRUTH

There are two species of children: yours and theirs.

Mother Murphy and her teenagers

TEEN LAW

The basic law of the mother/teenager relationship is that no teenager believes its mother to be a human being.

Early is to a mother what late is to a teenager.

MRS OSBERT'S FINDING

In the unlikely event that the entire family has gone out for the evening and you are watching a *very* good film, they will break down and be back, full of who did what and what the policeman said, just in time to drown the climax.

LAW OF THE FOND HEART
It is easier to love one's parents by letter.

LAW OF THE SUPERIOR TEENAGER
No woman will ever admit to having looked like the girls in the film her teenage children are whooping at. Twenty years will bring revenge.

ELSIE SMITH'S LAW OF HIGHER EDUCATION
If your child has the choice of two universities, three colleges and a specialist course in Europe, it will choose the wrong one. Somehow it will be your fault.

AUNT FLO'S DIG
It is hard to associate the boy with magenta hair with the studio portrait on the piano.

MOTHER MURPHY'S LAW
OF POLITE SONS

1. If your son is quiet, well groomed and good looking, he will come home one day with green spikes on his head, or scalp tattoos or whatever that year's male display plumage happens to be.
2. If your teenager gives no trouble at all he will decide to collect reptiles.
3. Everyone will tell you what an absolute *gentleman* your eighteen-year-old male chauvinist pig is.

MRS BROWN'S LAWS OF GOODBYE

1. Every time you wave goodbye to your child, there's a short pause, and it's back.
2. There are alternatives when the kids leave home: scribbled notes from the Afghan border; Sunday visits with huge amounts of baby laundry; having to put their old room to rights, as they are moving back.

P.S. (Kids are not all bad. The saddest thing to find among your souvenirs are the little spider-written notes: "We are sorry we broke the teapot. We love you.")

Marriage Murphology

MRS MURPHY'S MOST FUNDAMENTAL LAW OF MARRIAGE

The marriage ceremony cancels all previous attributes in any woman. The moment the ring is on her finger she automatically enjoys and is adept at cooking, cleaning windows, housework, ironing and cleaning the outside gutters.

MRS GORDON'S LAW OF ANXIETY

If you lie awake steeling yourself to have it out for once and for all, he'll be brought home in an ambulance.

NINA PEARCE'S LAW OF DISASTER

Men are always at a convention in San Francisco when the roof falls in.

MRS HACKENSACK'S BASIC LAW OF MARRIAGE

The man who marries to have children divorces his wife for giving them too much attention.

ASHTON'S OPENING GAMBIT

A woman wants a cup of coffee.
She goes out to the kitchen, puts the coffee maker on.
She calls out "Do you want a cup of coffee, dear?"

A man wants a cup of coffee.
He flings himself into his armchair.
He calls out "I'd like a cup of coffee, how about you, dear?"

Unless this is met early in the marriage with a strong answering gambit, the wife will be doomed to coffee-making into the twilight of senility, when here husband will upbraid her for boiling the percolator dry.

RUTH'S LAMENT

Women do not nag. They ask fifty times – because they get no response.

MAGGIE'S LAW

Women who apologise to keep the peace, get divorced for apologising all the time.

FAITH'S LAWS OF THE STRAYING HUSBAND

1. Mother Nature always sides with the other woman.
2. Men who leave home are astounded when their wives don't want them back.

MS JENKIN'S DEFINITIONS

Divorce is the act whereby two people are set free to begin again. He with his girlfriend, career, expense account and video. She with the kids, dog, cats, that funny clicking in the water pipes and a certificate for First Aid.

MS FREEDOM'S LAWS OF EXPERIENCE

1. Divorce is a tragedy that after a while feels suspiciously like relief.
2. A women only discovers that there is no magic in dealing with household bills when her husband has left her. All that solemn business with ruled columns and receipts can be successfully replaced by bills being paid as they come in.

MRS GREEN'S LAWS OF THE SINGLE PARENT

1. By the time you've saved for the carpet to go with the chairs, the chairs are worn out.
2. Children are ashamed to bring their friends home to the house they beat the hell out of.

Housework and drudgery laws

No one tells a woman when she marries the full range of what will be required of her. She really believes a fat recipe book and good baby and sex manual will cover everything. None of them deal with dying rabbits, the falling-in of doll's eyes, toilets stuffed with teddy bears and rice in the piano.

THE UNIVERSAL HOUSEWORK LAW
Housework expands to exclude all more interesting possibilities.

EVERY WIFE'S LAW
Housework takes longer than he thinks.

MOTHER-IN-LAW RULES
1. Every housewife has her blind spot. This will prove to be her mother-in-law's fetish.

FIRST LAW OF FISSION
There is always a piece missing from a clean break.

FIRST LAW OF THINGS
Things roll under things. And disappear.

THE LAWS OF IRONING

1. The huge linen tablecloth with lace inserts will eventually work its way to the top of the ironing pile.
2. Men rarely do the ironing. When they do, they practice on a brand new shirt.
3. Ironing boards were designed by men. Ironing boards bite.

MRS MORGAN'S THEORIES OF THE TIGHT SCHEDULE

1. If you can just make it to the bank if you trot, the old lady from next door will be going your way.
2. If there is only just time to complete a job, Jehovah's Witnesses will call.

MRS GOLIGHTLY'S LAW OF DESIGN

Any piece of equipment you buy after thorough research will at once become the subject of a design fault scandal.

MRS MURPHY'S FUNDAMENTAL LAW OF TIME-SAVING EQUIPMENT

The time saved by using a time-saving gadget is the amount of time required to clean and service it.

LAW OF UTILITY COMPANIES

Men from the gas, electricity or water companies never come twice. The second man to come will have no record of the first man's visit. The third man will be astonished that a woman knows so much about the technicalities.

MS MURPHY'S INSIGHTS

1. A man has been disadvantaged by being trained to believe that only the right tool can do any specific job. A woman has no such inhibitions.

2. Any woman knows that most repairs can be effected with
   a) a kitchen knife
   b) an unbent paperclip
   c) a comb
   d) soap
   e) a sharp blow

MACHINE LAW

The washing machine will, if a mother-in-law is expected, overflow and flood the kitchen: or it will overheat and grind to a halt when it is loaded with every spare shirt in the house.

My guarantee runs out in a week. Then we'll have some laughs!

BIDDY DANIEL'S LAW

If it is possible to make yourself look like a fool to an urgently summoned repair man, you will find the way.

Examples:

Non-operation of television set due to your not having put the plug in the socket.

Any item jammed solid with dust, as you did not know you had to clean it.

PAM'S LAW OF GANDALF'S GIFT

Children and cats have an instinct for the exact moment one is slipping luxuriantly into deep sleep. They choose this moment to be sick, shriek or put their paws in your eyes.

MRS BROWN'S LAW OF INSURANCE

You only discover you are not covered for flood when your house is three feet deep in water.

MRS FORSYTHE'S LAW

Any insurance you take out to cover your funeral expenses will, by the time you are dead, cover the cost of a bunch of dahlias.

LAW OF THE SALESMAN
When buying a house it should be borne in mind that the incidence of structural disaster is directly proportional to "charm".

JENNIFER'S LAW OF LATERAL TINKERING
Many a toilet has worked admirably for years with a hairbrush under the ball cock.

MRS GALLAGHER'S OBSERVATION ON POSSESSIONS

Books breed.

PAM'S THESES

1. There is a point in the space-time continuum that attracts keys and odd socks.
2. Objects are tidal. They flow in to fill the spaces behind any advancing housewife.

ANDREA'S LAW OF THE PERVERSE !?* STRING

When you have trimmed the string on a gift, you will discover something has been left out.
After untying the string, you will find it is no longer long enough to tie – and that there is no more string in the house.

TINKER'S LAWS

1. The difference between the amateur and the professional is that the professional tinkers boldly.
2. A good kick is the first recourse of any fixer, amateur or professional.

RULES OF THE OVER-ENTHUSIASTIC GARDENER

1. The coveted gift of a cutting with charming striped leaves will take two years of hard digging to uproot.
2. To the price of the sugar you need to make use of all that free fruit, add the cost of re-decorating the kitchen.

PAM BROWN'S FOUR BASIC CAT LAWS

1. If you need anything, a cat is sitting on it.
2. A cat in the house is a cat in the bed.
3. Cats walk very slowly in front of people carrying hot dishes.
4. People who say "Leave it long enough and he'll eat it", haven't got a cat.

Ms Murphy's consumerology

CHEESE LAW
The more varied the selection of cheeses the fewer varieties your guests will try.

LAW OF THE ELUSIVE BOOK
If you can't pay for the book today, the sales person, surrounded by copies, will assure you that there is no need for one to be put away for you. Tomorrow it will be out of print.

MS TIDY'S LAW
Yours new credit card is in the desk at home. This is the old one.

LAWS OF THE CLEVER PACKAGER
1. If a box boasts of its contents, "Added vitamins" the added vitamins are half the amount that were taken out by refining the original product.
2. "Home Baked" means factory baked, but lumpy.

MISS ANSTEY'S SHOPPING LIST LAWS

1. A shopping list is always complete, carefully considered and back home on the refrigerator.

2. The thing you don't bother to add to the shopping list as obvious, is the item you'll come home without.

LAW OF THE DISAPPEARING SALES PERSON

If you are just looking you will be harassed by sales people. Try to make a purchase in a hurry and they are all up a ladder or in the stockroom.

LAW OF THE STUPID CARPET REMNANTS

The carpet remnant you bought to the exact measurement of the room will need 6" off one way, and will be 8" short the other.

"HOPE SPRINGS ETERNAL" LAW

A woman dress-hunting looks first at the clothes she would have loved at 19, then at those designed for her age group, and finally at those she can get into.

PAM BROWN'S OBSERVATION

If the shoe is comfortable, it isn't fashionable.

LAW OF THE CLEVER ADVERTISER

The reason a TV washed sweater comes up looking like new is because it is.

LAW OF THE DASH TO THE SUPERMARKET

A sleepy corner grocer's will be packed with the entire street's kids if you rush to get a loaf of bread.

MS GRANT'S COROLLARY

Any line you join will move more slowly than any other, even if to all outward appearances it should be the fast-moving one. Which is why you joined it.

CORDELIA'S SHOPPING BAG LAW

When you're too tired to unpack the shopping before you've had a cup of tea, you've bought a large carton of ice cream.

MARY'S SECOND LAW OF THE DASH TO THE SUPERMARKET

In a bank the man in front of you will be having grave difficulties with his accounts.

In a Post Office he will be mailing a tarantula to the Czech Republic.

In a supermarket he will be shopping for a party of fifty guests.

JUNK LAW

Throw out that hideous green china dog and you will see its twin being sold in an antique shop.

HELEN'S COMPLAINT

Discover something odd and interesting in the attic and the dealer tells you that five years ago they were selling for a *fortune*.

MRS BROWN'S BOOK CLUB LAWS

Buy a book full price and it will at once be offered in your book club.

Buy it from your book club and it will at once become the introductory offer in your book club's sister club, at a fraction of the price.

Buy it in hard cover and it will come out in paperback.

MARY MONTAGUE'S CHINA LAWS

If you have broken something from your best set, the line has been discontinued or the manufacturer has gone bankrupt.

Final Blow: Five years later, just when you have given the remains away, you will find vast quantities of it at an auction.

THE BASIC LAWS OF RUMMAGE SALES

Nothing gets sent to a Charity Sale, except for a very good reason.

MRS BROWN'S COROLLARY

You will only find out what it was when you get it home.

MISS JONES' EMBARRASSMENT

The garment that reduces you and your friend
to hysterics was donated by the lady behind
the table.

SALLY STUART'S GENERALITY

All dresses at sales are size 10 – unless you wear
size 10, then they are size 20.

TILLY'S RULE

It is a proven fact that if you can't restrain the
impulse to buy an over-expensive article you have
lost your heart to, after a week it will be seen to be
shoddy, overpriced or the wrong shape.

Ms Murphy tries to cook

KATY CUSSON'S FINDING
The ingredients of an authentic peasant dish will cripple any budget outside its country of origin.

PAM'S EMBITTERMENT
If you, by accident, create a dish the entire family loves, you will never, ever be able to get it quite the same again.

MRS CUSSON'S GET-OUT
It is possible to leave the most expensive items out of a gourmet dish with no effect on its taste whatsoever.

JILLY'S' CULINARY DISASTER LAWS
1. Any dish that you have prepared a hundred times to universal acclaim, will fail disastrously when your boss comes to dinner.
2. Any dish that you have never prepared before will fail disastrously when your boss comes to dinner.

THREE LAWS OF THE IMPORTANT GUEST

1. In cooking, a mistake presented with conviction is a creation.
2. If your guest says the dish is interesting, it's a failure.
3. The pre-cooked and frozen dishes advocated by the experts as time-savers are the dishes found at the back of the refrigerator after the guests have gone home.

BERNADETTE'S BURN LAWS

1. There is no period of time whatsoever between dormant spaghetti, rice and milk and their eruption.
2. A casserole can progress from uncooked to burned without passing through singe.
3. The difference between raw and burned is going to the door to assure a gentleman you don't want a set of encyclopedia.

SUZIE'S DUMBO LAW

The most alarming occurrence in cooking is to find a basic ingredient on the table just as you've closed the oven door.

MOTHER MURPHY'S LAWS OF YUKKY OFFERINGS

1. The supreme test of mother love is a child-cooked breakfast.
2. A lemon meringue pie is never the same when it has been brought home in a school bag.

KAREN'S COMFORT

Children prefer cakes that have gone wrong.

MRS CUSSON'S LAW OF THE RUDE GUESTS

When you have spent the best part of a day in preparing supper for expected visitors they will arrive gasping, "Darling, *only* a cup of coffee! We broke down and ate a *huge* meal while we waited for the mechanic to do his thing!" At least they will not be coming again.

MOTHER HUBBARD'S LAWS

1. You only realize the ginger is cinnamon when you have promised the kids gingerbread men.
2. The lack of any vital ingredient means the supermarket is shut.

Ms Murphy in sickness and in health

MRS MOTHERWELL'S CONDENSED ENCYCLOPEDIA OF FAMILY HEALTH

1. Most women with pneumonia get it shopping with flu.
2. If there is an accident in the home, if any of the children are taken ill, or if the cat dies, your husband will be away on a business trip.
3. If your child is going to be ill, it will be ill in the middle of a vital examination.
4. Childhood diseases occur on a staggered principle. No two children will have them at the same time.

GRANNY'S SICK LAWS

1. The child who gallantly makes it to the bathroom, will throw up all over the pipes at the back.
2. The child who says he's going to throw up, is going to throw up.

LAWS OF THE STRONGER SEX

1. Husbands sleep through all 2 a.m. situations, from a child's initial cough through the increasing wail, the clatter of bowls, the running of water, the search for clean nightclothes, the stripping of sheets, the remaking of beds, the positioning of towels, buckets and glasses of water and the subsequent goodnights, the running of the bath and the reek of disinfectant. They are astonished and a little rattled by the fact their breakfast is late.

2. Men are the stronger sex, so long as they are not required to deal with vomit, blood, puddles, poos or snotty noses. This is women's work, and no Ph.D can save her from it.

MOTHER MURPHY VINDICATED

Any woman who goes to the doctor with a sore toe and her bra held together with safety pins, will be told he'd like to examine her chest.

LAW OF THE CHAUVINIST DOCTOR'S DIAGNOSIS

It's your age. (Then why is my other leg so darned healthy?)

THE BOSS'S WORKING RULES

1. All female illness is based on the menstrual cycle. Coming. Late. Present. Dragging on. Going. Gone at Last. Coming.
2. Depression in women is caused by the time of the month. Depression in men is caused by unprecedented stress.

THE LAW OF RANDOM STRIKE

The stomach that remains silent in the 1812 Overture erupts in the quieter passages of the Mozart.

DOCTOR'S COMFORT

Modern drugs are wonderful. They enable a wife with pneumonia to nurse her husband through flu.

MRS SMITH'S HOMELY OBSERVANCES

Any cut, burn, scald or scrape on the hand will be exactly where it will be aggravated by the maximum number of household tasks.

Beauty and the laws of growing old

BARBARA'S OBSERVATIONS
1. Garlic outlasts Chanel.
2. The scent that smelled like Paris on her, smells like fly spray on you.

JANET SWAN'S LAWS OF DRESS DISASTERS
1. If you are asked out suddenly, your only decent dress is hanging, dripping, over the bath.
2. The reason you felt so comfortable all evening is because your zipper was undone.
3. The woman striding out, her hands deep in her pockets, is holding up her panties.
4. The most wonderful evening of your life is wiped out when you realize you experienced it with two different shoes.
5. If everyone seems to be sharing your feeling of elation, it's because you've lost the eyelashes off one eye.

FAT FREDA'S LAMENT

Plate glass windows tell you what the bathroom mirror doesn't.

LAW OF THE DIET

If you wean yourself off fat, you will get hooked on wholewheat cereal and become even fatter.

LAWS OF THE BULGE

1. Youth is the time when the stomach and chest occupy different parts of the body.
2. There comes a time when only you can tell when you are pulling in your tummy.

LAWS OF HAIRDRESSING FAILURES

1. Your most expensive hairdo ever, will look like a wig.
2. Hairdressers always take stunned horror for ecstasy.

ANDRE'S LAW

Madam has always got difficult hair.

RUTH'S REGRETS

1. There comes a day when a man putting his arm round you to help you over an obstacle is just kind.
2. To a man of any age a woman over forty is past it.

FIRST RULE OF THE HAIR SALON
No hairdresser ever believes their client knows what she wants.

LAW OF THE MATURING VIRAGO
A man is as old as he feels.
A woman is as old as she looks.

MRS FLANNERY'S LAMENT
The well-preserved woman looks just that.

COROLLARIES
1. Lipstick applied over the lipline to give an illusion of youth, looks like lipstick applied over the lipline to give an illusion of youth.
2. The better the youth restoring job, the older people imagine you must be.

LAW OF THE MUMMIFIED BEAUTY QUEEN
Only an expert can tell one rich Californian woman from another as they all use the same plastic surgeon.

Young Miss Murphy sets out

TAMMY'S LAWS OF THE PIMPLE

1. For the teenager the embodiment of Murphy's Law is The Pimple.
2. New dress from the catalogue? New boyfriend calling in his newly-sprayed Porsche to haul you off to the Disco? There it is. The Pimple.
3. All afternoon The Pimple lies dormant, a faint pink splotch, but then with half an hour to go, it erupts into life, pulsing like a generator, luminescent, inescapable. Nothing on God's earth is going to hide it.

THE LAW ACCORDING TO AUNT SALLY

If The Pimple doesn't get you, The Period will.

CINDY'S LAW

The only really cool shoes are the ones designed for people with only four toes.

POLLYANNA'S LAW OF THE ROAD TO HELL
When that nice old lady over the road asks you to post a vital letter, you experience a pleasant holy glow. You find it in your handbag a week later.

TV RULE
There is never a pop concert on TV unless Dad's sport is on the other channel.

TIMID TILLY'S FASHION LAW
You look like a middle-aged lady. So you have your hair dyed green and cut into a Mohican. You wear six pairs of earrings and black lipstick.... You look like a middle-aged lady with a Mohican.

THE EXPENSIVE CLOTHES LAW
It costs more to look dishevelled.

COMING DOWN TO EARTH WITH A BANG LAW
It's very difficult to look convincingly trendy when you're eight months pregnant.

DOT'S FASHION PARANOIAS

1. Murphy's Law means that you will be reduced to dreadful embarrassment if you try clothes on in boutiques.

2. If it's an open changing room, it will either be full of huge bronzed ladies, or dark slim girls who look terrific in everything they try on.

3. If it's a private changing cubicle, the very moment you have zipped your hair into the skirt and are locked double, or have zipped your panties into the skirt and are trying to loosen them with your teeth; the very moment when you have managed to get both legs down on one side of culottes, or when you are simply standing there in your safety pins and knotted shoulder straps – at that moment an elegant, exquisitively groomed woman will poke her head through the curtains and ask, "Do you need any help, Madam?"

Miss Murphy leaves home

THE FUNDAMENTAL LAW OF LEAVING HOME

She who thinks she was paying her mother far too much for her keep sooner or later finds she wasn't.

LANDLADY LAWS

1. You've been complaining for six months about the gas cooker. The landlady at last comes to take a look at it. It works perfectly. The next day a blow back takes off your eyebrows.
2. The kindly landlady who only asks for Reasonable Access is the one who is going to read all your correspondence and rifle through your underwear drawers.
3. Asking a landlady to get anything repaired is like playing Russian roulette. One shot gives you a new water heater, the other five weeks' notice.

SUKIE'S WANT ADS PROVISO

The Third Girl, who looks like a gift from heaven, is the one who turns out to be hell. Unless you are the Third Girl, when it's the other two.

BEWARE THE GERM FREAK LAW

You always wanted a nice clean room mate. Now you've got one. And all the food tastes of bleach.

PAULINE'S LAW OF PEBBLES AT MIDNIGHT

Your insomniac room mate will be deep, deep, deeply asleep the night you forget your key.

PATSY'S TWO'S COMPANY LAW

The night you ask him in for coffee is the night your room mate will forget it was her turn to go to bed early. She won't be able to go to bed then because it would look too obvious. So you'll talk politics till dawn.

PRISCILLA'S ADVICE ON PREARRANGEMENT

Ask him in for coffee and your room mate has forgotten to buy any. Look for the red wine and find she's celebrated with her boyfriend: this is confirmed by the dishes in the sink and the guffaws coming from her room.

BESSY'S FIRST WARNING

If you share with a biologist, don't eat anything in the refrigerator.

BESSY'S SECOND WARNING

Any vegetarian room mate can eventually make you feel you knew your steak personally.

MARY'S LAW

Room mates never notice the desperate note that says, "Urgent. Get three extra pints of milk and one pint of cream for party".

A GIRL'S HOUSE IS HER CASTLE LAW

When you ask your new heart throb into the living room, you'll remember one second too late that you've been cutting your toenails.

JENNY BUTT'S LAWS OF LOST FACE

1. Sophisticated friends only turn up at your house when you've gone to bed with a mug of cocoa at eight o'clock.
2. Unexpected guests mean nothing but baked beans and half a packet of stale cookies in the place.
3. Mothers only turn up unexpectedly the day after a party, and before you've had time to move the bodies.

Ms Murphy goes out to work

JOB HUNTER'S LORE
It always rains on the way to an interview

COROLLARIES
1. If you find a parking-space in front of the office, the interview will take place in an annexe, two blocks away.
2. Always take the kitchen drawer to an interview. Your references are in it.
3. If you turn up at an interview dressed in one red and blue shoe, don't worry. You have an identical pair at home.

LAW OF JOB INEQUALITY
No matter how efficient senior members of staff may be, women will continue to be judged on the length of time the most junior spend in the powder room.

MS MURPHY'S COROLLARIES TO THE LAW OF INEQUALITY
1. Criminals hate to be apprehended by small, pretty policewomen.

2. People are always astonished when a young female lawyer gets them off.

3. If you've written, painted, sculpted, composed, directed or arranged anything with professional skill and some authority, the highest praise you can hope for is to have someone say they had *no* idea you were a woman.

L.M.'S WARNING
Never be alone in the office with the man who has religious tracts in his desk.

NINA'S RULE
If a woman is told her work is indispensable, it usually means she's going to go on being underpaid.

MELISSA'S LAW OF THE OLD BAG
No matter how intelligent, smart, efficient and experienced a woman is, if she's over forty, she's an old bag.

MELISSA'S COMPENSATION LAW

Any intelligent, smart, efficient and experienced woman over forty is promoted.

NAUGHTY BOSS WARNING

When the boss lets his hair down at the office party, make sure it's not your panties that go with it.

TOOTSIE'S LAW

She who addresses her male boss as he addresses her is asking for trouble... "Sweetheart", "Goldilocks", "Janet-dear".

BASIC LAWS OF THE FEMALE EXECUTIVE

1. However highly qualified, however intelligent and experienced, a woman in business must be regarded as A Risk, as her mind will be occupied by Personal Concerns.
2. Any successful businesswoman is believed to henpeck her husband.

CATCH 22 LAWS OF THE FEMALE EXECUTIVE

Men don't like women with briefcases.
Men don't like women who don't take their job seriously.

SALLY'S FINAL RETORT: THE STRUCTURAL LAW OF HIERARCHY

The lady who makes the coffee rules the office.

SECOND CATCH 22 LAW

Men admire women who are intelligent, independent and outspoken. They even believe they should be promoted. They just don't like working with women who are intelligent, independent and outspoken.

MRS J. C. BEALE'S LAWS OF THE PROMOTED FEMALE

1. Women talking together are gossiping. Men talking together are keeping a finger on the pulse.
2. The man who spends a great part of the working day in bars and restaurants is Making Useful Contacts. The woman who goes home at lunch time to see how the kids are Simply Hasn't Her Heart In Her Work.

OLD ADAGE

Behind every boss is an able woman.

1990'S COROLLARY

Under any boss is a stupid woman.

MS JENNY KENT'S LAW
The size of the ladder depends exactly on the importance of the deal.

MS HAZELL'S SHORT LAW FOR SENIOR EXECUTIVES
If you are the only woman on the board it's your fault if there's no coffee.

FAITH'S LAW OF RIGHT AND WRONG
When you are wrong, the boss never forgets. When you are right, he or she takes the credit.

THE LAW OF THE LATE, LATE JUNIOR SECRETARY
If you tell the boss you are late because of a train derailment, the next day there will be a train derailment.

COROLLARIES
1. Trains are never derailed on the boss's line.
2. The only time you have a genuine excuse the reason will be so extravagantly implausible it will be useless to present it.

BASIC LAW OF TYPING

Cups of coffee are valued more highly than typing speeds.

MS KENT'S LAW

Word Processors crash only on busy days and Friday afternoons.

MERCIA'S LAW

The idiot who decides to gulp a quick lunch at her desk is the one available for emergency dictation.

THE PACKAGE LAW

The moment you have finished wrestling that slithery role of film into a tough cardboard tube, wrapped it in acres of stiff brown paper and swaddled it in yards of voraciously sticky tape, your boss will want it sent in a flat cardboard box.

LETTERS OF THE LORE

The letter the boss wants retyped is always the last letter of the day.
This letter is always the longest.
The last letter is the most urgent.
The most urgent letter gets put in the wrong envelope.

Ms Murphy in love

PAM'S RATHER BASIC OBSERVATION
The difference between reality and romance is indigestion.

PAT'S PRACTICALITY
A Grand Passion rarely survives a stuck zipper.

DIANA'S LAW OF SHORT STRAWS
The evening you wear five inch heels on a blind date, he is five foot three.

MS LAING'S PRINCE CHARMING LAWS
1. If he's charming, sophisticated, handsome, he'll turn out to have an extensive collection of tarantulas in his bedroom.
2. He's handsome. He's kind. He's intelligent. He's gay.

PAM'S POST-SCRIPT
Women exist to keep men's sports equipment clean.

MISS DURBAN'S LAWS OF THE ONE-THAT-GOT-AWAY

1. The man who lights up the party for you is going Bahrain for two years. Tomorrow.
2. The man whose eyes meet yours is always on the other platform.
3. If you've saved for four weeks of sun and roman with your boyfriend, you'll meet the love of your life the day before you fly.

KITTY'S KITSCH LAW

If he can ever be persuaded to window shop he'll make wonderfully witty remarks about the incredib vulgarity of the objects displayed. You'll have one a home, done up in navy blue paper with little gold stars, with his name on it.

POLLY'S LAWS OF THE JINXED COURTSHI

1. If you are still in your bathrobe, uncombed and unwashed and eating peanut butter and jelly sandwiches at half past eleven in the morning, t guy you thought was in Japan will turn up.
2. When you spend all afternoon arranging the lig the furniture, the food, the wine and yourself, h come through the door gasping, "Just made it", walk straight past you and switch on the TV.

Ms Murphy and the macho man

FAITH'S FIRST LAW
Mother Nature is a male chauvinist pig.

THE DUAL ASPECT RULE
Men get wet, muddy and exhausted pursuing excitement.
Women get wet, muddy and exhausted doing the weekly shopping.

BASIC TRUTH
Only men get flu. Women get colds.

MRS MURPHY'S MUCKY LAWS
Men do not deal with vomit.

"A WOMAN'S PLACE..." LAW
A man sprawled in a chair is recharging his batteries.
A woman sprawled in a chair is neglecting her duties.
Corollary: A woman doing nothing is a guilty woman.

MRS PETER'S DESIGN OBSERVATION

Men have been so far the most active in design. They have succeeded in building houses with no space for an ironing board, stores without escalators, stations with no ramps for wheelchairs, high rise accommodation that sends the inhabitants insane, shopping trolleys with permanently jammed wheels and kitchen cabinets too high for anyone to reach.

FINAL STRAW

Men get time off work for illness.

PAM'S ANTI-NUCLEAR LAW

Any woman preoccupied with trying to stop the destruction of the planet is irresponsible. And a lesbian.

MRS PETER'S ARCHITECTURAL OBSERVATION

Only a man could have designed the Corbusier Machines for Living.
Women are the people who have nervous breakdowns living in them.

MRS PLATO'S LAW
Men, when they die, hope to discover the riddle of the Universe.
Women hope to find out where odd socks go.

MRS EINSTEIN'S CHIP
Men love to work out problems on graph paper – and then cannot resist translating them into actuality. This process has given us the Theory of Relativity, Calculus, Marxism, Nazism, the nuclear bomb and the silicon chip.
Women do little sums on the backs of envelopes and have, so far, ensured the continuation of the human race.

MS DAVENPORT'S LAWS OF THE LITTLE WOMAN
1. The woman whom a man marries for her intelligence and originality is the one he will divorce for being too smart for her own good.
2. Men regard their women knowing more than they do on any subject at a dinner party as an insult to their manhood and an act of disloyalty.

MRS MURPHY'S DOUBLE VISION
Men sow their wild oats. Women are sluts.
Men are always flabbergasted when the girl gets
pregnant.

Ms Murphy on sex

AVRIL'S BASIC LAW OF SEX

Homo sapiens like to make everything more
difficult – getting food out of wrappers, starting
toilet paper rolls, tearing foil without ripping the
hand to the bone, sex.

MS WILLIAM'S BEDROOM ETIQUETTE

"I've got a headache" is a synonym for "You reek
of beer."

MS KNOTT'S OBSERVATIONS ON SEX

The greatest drawback in a passionate affair is
being ticklish.

The higher primates have evolved probably the
clumsiest method of procreation in the universe.
And no amount of poetry is going to change it.

CRUMBY PROVERB

1. Pleasantly blurred by wine you sink down in front of the fire – and on to the jagged edges of the only hazelnut shell to have escaped the vacuum.
2. You'd forgotten you had on thermal underwear.
3. He hasn't shaved. Again.

HOUSEWIVE'S LAW OF SEX

It is a devastating example of Ms Murphy's Law that as you spiral to orgasm you will remember you haven't turned the gas off under the coffee pot.

GERMAINE'S PARTING SHOT

No orgasm is just one more thing to add to the average woman's guilt complex.

MS KEEPING'S LAW OF REALITY

1. A woman weeping after making love may well be a woman laughing herself silly.
2. Sex is a biological function that simply evolved for the continuation of the species. You'd never guess.

3. The biggest turn-off in the world is a man working his way through the erogenous zones according to the manual.